You Are There

Pompeii 79

Wendy Conklin, M.A.

Consultants

Timothy Rasinski, Ph.D.
Kent State University

Lori Oczkus, M.A.
Literacy Consultant

Publishing Credits

Rachelle Cracchiolo, M.S.Ed., *Publisher*
Conni Medina, M.A.Ed., *Managing Editor*
Dona Herweck Rice, *Series Developer*
Emily R. Smith, M.A.Ed., *Content Director*
Stephanie Bernard/Susan Daddis, M.A.Ed., *Editors*
Robin Erickson, *Senior Graphic Designer*

The TIME logo is a registered trademark of TIME Inc. Used under license.

Image Credits: Cover and p.1 Purix Verlag Volker Christen/
Bridgeman Images; pp.10–11 © Look and Learn/Bridgeman Images;
all other images from iStock and/or Shutterstock.

Library of Congress Cataloging-in-Publication Data

Names: Conklin, Wendy, author.
Title: You are there! Pompeii 79 / Wendy Conklin, M.A.
Description: Huntington Beach, CA : Teacher Created Materials, [2017]|
    Includes index. | Audience: Grades 7-8.
Identifiers: LCCN 2016034995 (print) | LCCN 2016035397 (ebook) | ISBN
    9781493836154 (pbk.) | ISBN 9781480757196 (eBook)
Subjects: LCSH: Pompeii (Extinct city)--Juvenile literature. | Vesuvius
    (Italy)--Eruption, 79--Juvenile literature.
Classification: LCC DG70.P7 C6245 2017 (print) | LCC DG70.P7 (ebook)
    | DDC
    937/.7256807--dc23
LC record available at https://lccn.loc.gov/2016034995

Teacher Created Materials

5301 Oceanus Drive
Huntington Beach, CA 92649-1030
http://www.tcmpub.com

ISBN 978-1-4938-3615-4

Table of Contents

Prologue: Unknown Dangers 4

Morning Calm 5

Afternoon Chaos 14

Evening Escape 24

The Next Morning .26

Epilogue: Buried in Time 27

Glossary 28

Index 29

Check It Out! 30

Try It! 31

About the Author 32

Prologue:
Unknown Dangers

Long ago, in a bustling village near the Bay of Naples in Italy, tragedy struck. Mount Vesuvius, a volcano on the edge of Pompeii, had been **dormant** for about 800 years, slowly building pressure. The people of Pompeii could not have anticipated that the volcano would erupt on August 24, 79. But when the earth shook and ash rained from the sky, the city was doomed. This is a story of how a resident of Pompeii—a fictional barber—may have experienced the explosion of Mount Vesuvius.

The Signs of an Eruption

Several days before Mount Vesuvius erupted, tremors shook the town of Pompeii. Doors creaked, glasses shook, and hanging light fixtures swung back and forth. Springs and wells in the area dried up. It appears that many Pompeians ignored these signs because they had experienced them before.

Morning Calm

8:00 a.m.

The creaking door wakes you again this morning. Didn't you fix the door frame yesterday? Let's face it: being a barber doesn't necessarily make you a very good carpenter. You've got to get up anyway and make your way down to the **forum** early, so you can set up shop in a good location. Lately, Pompeians haven't been stopping by for shaves, much less haircuts. That old barber, Flavius, has been landing the ideal location under the **colonnade**, but you have to beat him to that spot today. Your rent is due soon, and you need to make money to keep living in your tiny apartment.

There are about 20,000 people living here in Pompeii, and it feels as if they all reside on your street. The noise of children crying and the stench of rotting food dumped out in the streets make this living arrangement miserable (especially now, in the heat of August). The only thing worse than this would be living above the **bathhouse**. Having to listen to men splashing water around and singing at the tops of their lungs would drive anyone mad.

Do Animals Have a Sixth Sense?

On the day of the eruption in Pompeii, animals might have behaved strangely. There's no proof that animals can sense things before they happen. But scientists think that animals can hear **infrasonic** sounds, such as the rumbling of the earth before an earthquake. So, they would react by fleeing.

8:30 a.m.

You better be careful where you walk in the **cobblestone** streets. The garbage is everywhere, and there's no chance of rain to wash it all away. What you wouldn't give to have some sewers around this place! Your neighbor's bird is making odd chirping noises and trying to get out of its cage—very strange behavior for such a content bird.

You know you're out of wine, fish, eggs, and bread, so you better stop by the tavern on your way to the forum and get something to eat. The Vulcan holiday celebrated yesterday has ended, and things can get back to business as usual.

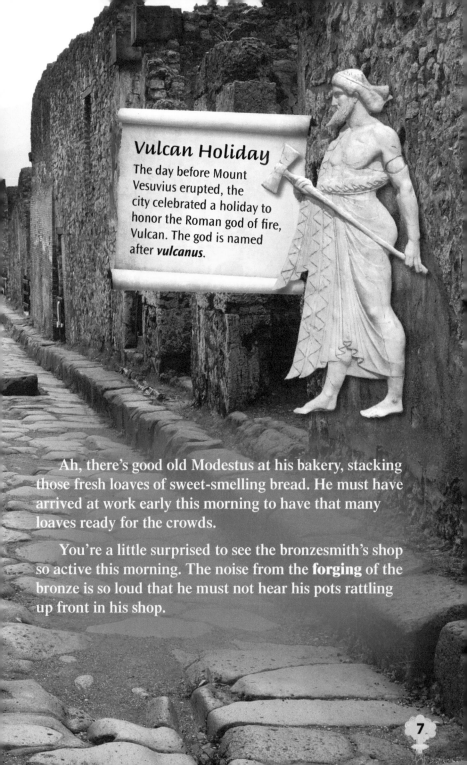

Vulcan Holiday

The day before Mount Vesuvius erupted, the city celebrated a holiday to honor the Roman god of fire, Vulcan. The god is named after *vulcanus*.

Ah, there's good old Modestus at his bakery, stacking those fresh loaves of sweet-smelling bread. He must have arrived at work early this morning to have that many loaves ready for the crowds.

You're a little surprised to see the bronzesmith's shop so active this morning. The noise from the **forging** of the bronze is so loud that he must not hear his pots rattling up front in his shop.

9:00 a.m.

Finally, you arrive at the tavern, eager for a dish of steaming vegetable stew. You take a seat at the counter, which is already filled with jars of snacks such as olives, breads, and cheeses. You catch the eye of your usual server, Atia, and she's off to get your favorite red wine from the **amphora** in the back of the tavern. Not the most expensive wine, though . . . she knows your budget.

Belief in Spirits

In Pompeii, it was common for a home or a business to have a **lararium** to honor the spirits they believed provided protection. Some lararia were simple paintings. For the wealthy residents, they were more elaborate, with statues in small temples.

You glance over at the painting of the **lares** on the wall next to the counter. Shrines like these can be found on almost every building, and Pompeians believe the shrines will protect them. You place a few **sesterces** in the jar on the counter to take care of your bill and head to the forum to get ready for the day.

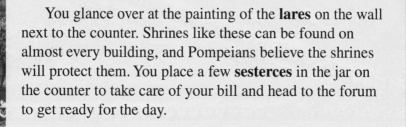

A Busy City

Before the eruption in AD 79, Pompeii was bustling with residents and tourists. Streets were lined with shops, cafes, and bathhouses. There were two theaters; the larger one hosted gladiator fights, which were popular at the time.

10:00 a.m.

The streets are especially crowded today, which tells you that the forum is going to be busy. You enter the forum and pass the Temple of Jupiter first. Statius, a well-known poet, is entertaining the crowd with his latest poem. The majestic horse statues in front of the temple take your breath away every time you see them, but you rarely have time to reflect. You need to get to work. Busy priests pass by, and there's Publius heading into his office above the grain warehouse. You see he's wearing a new robe; business must be good.

Shop Is Open!

People selling goods and services (such as barbers) set up shop in the colonnade. Busy merchants, politicians, and businessmen stopped by to get what they needed for the day.

Temple of Apollo before the eruption

As a barber, you hear the gossip about people living in Pompeii, such as how the banker Lucius is taking Gaius, the **fuller**, to court for an unpaid loan. They are standing in front of the **basilica** now, and it looks as though a politician on the steps has a large crowd listening to his speech—those politicians always have something to say. You find a good spot under the colonnade and set up your chair, table, and equipment.

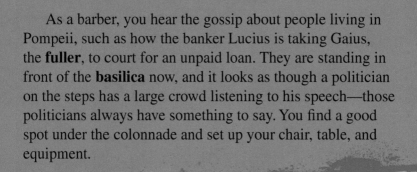

THINK LINK

◎ How is life today similar to life in Pompeii in 79? How is it different?

◎ Based on what you know, what type of job would you prefer in Pompeii?

Temple of Apollo after the eruption

11:00 a.m.

Your first customer of the day, the town **philosopher**, stops by for a shave. He asks if you felt the earth shake this morning. You remark that Pompeii isn't done rebuilding after the last time the gods shook the ground 17 years ago. The philosopher informs you that despite what you and your fellow Pompeians believe, there may be another explanation, but you can't help wondering if the gods are angry with the people of Pompeii again after the rumblings of the past few days.

A Terrible Earthquake

In AD 62, an earthquake shook the city of Pompeii. The earthquake was the result of **magma** shifting inside the mountain and making its way closer to the top.

12:55 p.m.

You hear other bits of news as the morning passes, and you decide to step away from the colonnade to take a break. Should you go down to the theater to watch the newest play? No, you would rather go to the bathhouse and exercise instead.

It's a Volcano, All Right!

The Romans believed Mount Vesuvius was an **extinct** volcano. Because there had not been any eruptions recorded in 800 years, the people of Pompeii felt they had no need to worry. They didn't understand that earthquakes could be connected to volcanic eruptions.

Afternoon Chaos

12:59 p.m.

As you walk through the forum, you notice a crowd of people gathered around the public fountain. You move closer and notice the fountain is no longer flowing with water. Others around you seem equally puzzled by the sight. You look at one another in confusion until your attention is pulled away—and the world comes crashing down.

1:00 p.m.

Vibrations rattle through your body, and you realize something's about to happen. An explosion flings your body to the ground. You're astonished to see a fiery, dust-filled cloud rising from the mountain. As if in slow motion, the temple walls and the colonnade shake and buildings collapse throughout the forum. You stumble to your feet and dodge the tiles plummeting from the roofs of nearby buildings. Where should you go, and what should you do?

You realize that, first, you need to go home and gather your valuables—you're not going to let some **pilferers** take what little you have. A dark cloud is rising higher and higher in the sky over the mountain. You're not sure what it means, but you know it's **ominous**. You steady your legs and make your way down the narrow streets.

The Cloud on Mount Vesuvius

When Vesuvius erupted, a column of ash, pumice, and rock rose 12 miles (19 kilometers) into the air. It only took half an hour for the pumice and ash to reach Pompeii, which was about 6 miles (10 kilometers) away.

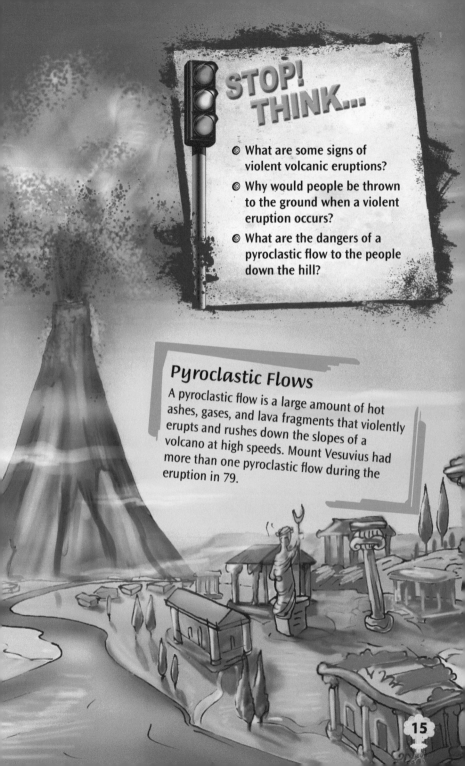

STOP! THINK...

- What are some signs of violent volcanic eruptions?
- Why would people be thrown to the ground when a violent eruption occurs?
- What are the dangers of a pyroclastic flow to the people down the hill?

Pyroclastic Flows

A pyroclastic flow is a large amount of hot ashes, gases, and lava fragments that violently erupts and rushes down the slopes of a volcano at high speeds. Mount Vesuvius had more than one pyroclastic flow during the eruption in 79.

1:30 p.m.

Amidst all the chaos, you reach your house and find everything is still intact, except for a few pieces of broken pottery on the floor—the result of the shaking. You go straight to the lararium and secure the family statuettes that honor the gods. You grab some figs from the table, gather a few family valuables and your money in a bag, and quickly head back outside. You must get to the shore so you can board a ship and sail to Misenum until it's safe to return.

You step outside, and the darkness engulfs you so completely that you can't see anything. Something hard hits your shoulder, and you realize it's **lapilli** falling from the sky. You duck as rocks rain from above. Your neighbor yells to take cover, but you think it's safer to leave town rather than take shelter. You slowly feel your way down the street in the direction of the Bay of Naples. A whining dog chained to a pole outside a house grabs your attention. His owners didn't take the time to unleash him, so you quickly remove the collar and set him free.

Grab Your Pillow

Many people in Pompeii and in neighboring towns needed to protect their heads from the lapilli. According to one man's account, many people tied pillows onto their heads.

Rocks from the Sky

Lapilli can be dangerous. They can range from less than 1 inch to 2.5 inches (6.4 centimeters) in diameter. Lapilli from the eruption were found only in Pompeii even though Herculaneum was closer to the volcano.

2:00 p.m.

It's difficult to see, so it's going to take a while to get to the bay. Others struggle to carry trunks full of valuables, and you wonder if it's worth trying to save such things. White ash covers everything and everyone. As the minutes tick by, the ash piles deeper and deeper in the streets, lightning flashes in the sky near the mountain, and people cry out to the gods. Others yell that the world is coming to an end as the noise of the rocks hitting the roofs grows louder. The terror in their voices only makes you more determined to leave Pompeii.

People scream as a roof nearby collapses beneath the weight of the falling rocks. It doesn't look like any people inside could have survived. You cover your mouth with your robe to keep from breathing in the ash and dust as you continue feeling your way toward the port.

Prized Possessions

After the initial eruption, many Pompeians ran to gather their belongings. Among them were valuable items such as jewelry and coins. Other people carried charms, rings, and objects meant to provide luck or protection.

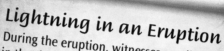

Lightning in an Eruption

During the eruption, witnesses saw lightning in the sky near the volcano. This happens when lava fragments rub against each other in an ash cloud and static electricity builds up. The electrical charge releases bolts into the cloud and creates lightning.

2:15 p.m.

You finally make it to the bay and can see ships in the distance. Could this be the navy fleet from Misenum coming to rescue Pompeians? People desperately yell for the ships to land, but the port is dark, and sailors with the fleet can't see the struggling people on land. The violent waves bring in volcanic **debris** that litters the shore. Your heart sinks as you realize that even if the ships could find you, it's impossible for them to land.

A Navy Fleet to the Rescue

Pliny the Elder was the commander of the navy stationed in Misenum. After seeing the eruption, he took the fleet so he could rescue people. It was difficult for him to see the port in the darkness, and the debris made it impossible to land there.

3:00 p.m.

A few small boats are abandoned on the beach, and you consider jumping into one and escaping this nightmare. But the strong, violent winds won't allow the boats to leave shore. Taking cover in a nearby boathouse with others seems to be the best option. You hope the chaos ends soon.

Pliny's Account of the Eruption

Pliny the Younger was the nephew of Pliny the Elder, the commander of the naval fleet stationed in Misenum. Pliny the Younger wrote many letters describing various events and occurrences throughout his lifetime. He was only 18 years old when Mount Vesuvius erupted. His description is the only firsthand account of this event. Here are excerpts from his writings about that momentous day.

On the 24th of August, about one in the afternoon, my mother desired him [Pliny's uncle] to observe a cloud, which appeared of a very unusual size and shape. He immediately arose and went out upon a rising ground from whence he might get a better sight of this very uncommon appearance. A cloud, from which mountain was uncertain, at this distance (but it was found afterwards to come from Mount Vesuvius), was ascending, the appearance of which i cannot give you a more exact description of than by likening it to that of a pine tree, for it shot up to a great height in the form of a very tall trunk, which spread itself out at the top into a sort of branches; occasioned, i imagine, either by a sudden gust of air that impelled it, the force of which decreased as it advanced upwards, or the cloud itself being pressed back again by its own weight, expanded in the manner i have mentioned; it appeared sometimes bright and sometimes dark and spotted, according as it was either more or less impregnated with earth and cinders. This phenomenon seemed to a man of such learning and research as my uncle extraordinary and worth further looking into.

Pliny the Elder's Fate

Pliny the Elder landed at Pompeii. Once there, he bathed and slept in an attempt to keep those around him calm. When he awakened, he went to the shore to determine how to flee the danger. He was overcome with fumes. Pliny the Younger wrote, "his body was found intact and uninjured, still fully clothed and more like sleep than death."

Pliny the Elder ordered his fleet to go ashore to rescue the people trapped in the city. Here's Pliny the Younger's account of what happened while in the Bay of Naples.

He was now so close to the mountain that the cinders, which grew thicker and hotter the nearer he approached, fell into the ships, together with pumice-stones, and black pieces of burning rock: they were in danger too not only of being aground by the sudden retreat of the sea, but also from the vast fragments which rolled down from the mountain, and obstructed all the shore.

Pliny the Younger, Translated by William Melmoth [revised by F. C. T. Bosanquet]

Evening Escape

4:00 p.m.

People around you are wheezing and coughing from breathing the ash. You realize it's not safe to stay in Pompeii. You head out into the street and make your way to the Sarno River, hoping the **wharfs** there will be the answer to your rescue. Unfortunately, the river is blocked by debris.

Through the ash, you look around to see other people gathered here with their riches and livestock, hoping for a boat to take them to safety. Knowing you have to find another way out of here, you see an abandoned donkey and jump on its back. With the winds blowing in the direction of Pompeii, the best chance for survival is in Herculaneum, a city to the northwest.

plaster cast of a victim of Mount Vesuvius

7:00 p.m.

Surprisingly, ash has not covered Herculaneum. Lightning illuminates the mountain, and an enormous cloud is rising from it. Despite the people who believe this is a safe place, it is actually closer to the mountain than Pompeii. You decide to press on toward Misenum. If you make good time, you can be there by morning.

August 25, 12:01 a.m.

A roaring avalanche shakes the ground in the darkness, and you hear faraway screams, most likely from Herculaneum. In a matter of seconds, the screams have quieted. You must reach Misenum, as it's your only hope for safety.

Volcanic Mudslide

On August 25, shortly after midnight, the first pyroclastic flow hit Herculaneum, instantly killing the remaining townspeople. After the surge, a volcanic mudslide overtook the entire town, burying it for 1,500 years.

The Next Morning

6:30 a.m.

You join other refugees in Misenum, some of whom are from Pompeii. Amidst the wheezing and coughing, you share stories as you look to the mountain in the distance and see it is still shrouded in darkness. The ground begins to shake again, and a glowing fire suddenly rushes down the slopes toward Pompeii.

As you look at the bay, the water on the shore rushes backward, and just as suddenly as the shaking began, it ends in silence, and the ash begins to fall in Misenum.

You can never go back to your home in Pompeii—the ash and rocks cover everything. The residents in Misenum panic as they pack up and head farther west. There is no choice but to follow them, as there is no future in the shadow of Mount Vesuvius.

Epilogue: Buried in Time

By 6:30 a.m., the last pyroclastic flow had rushed down the mountain to Pompeii. The hot gases burned people's lungs and killed them instantly. Pompeii was buried and forgotten. That is until the 1700s, when it was discovered by a peasant digging a well. This finding helped launch an **excavation** of Pompeii. Today, only about 60 percent of Pompeii has been excavated.

More Survivors Than Not

Historians believe Pompeii had a population of about 20,000 people at the time of the eruption. Archaeologists have uncovered only 1,150 skeletons, so they believe that many of the residents made it out alive.

Glossary

amphora—a container for storing wine

basilica—a building in the forum that was used as a courthouse and for public meetings

bathhouse—a public building equipped with hot and cold baths, a pool, a changing room, and a gymnasium

cobblestone—round stone that was used to pave streets

colonnade—a row of columns that hold up a roof

debris—the remains or ruins of broken things

dormant—a volcano that has not erupted in some time but may erupt again in the future

excavation—an area where dirt and stones are removed to uncover something beneath

extinct—a volcano that will not erupt again

forging—making or shaping a metal object by heating and hammering it

forum—a public square or marketplace

fuller—a person who works with cloth

infrasonic—relating to sound waves that are at a lower frequency than can be heard by the human ear

lapilli—rock fragments formed when magma is ejected from a volcano

lararium—a shrine for the spirits in a person's home

lares—household spirits that protected families

magma—melted rock under Earth's surface

ominous—threatening; menacing

philosopher—a person who studies knowledge and truth and offers ideas on the questions of life

pilferers—thieves or looters

sesterces—silver coins from ancient Roman times

vulcanus—the Latin term for volcano

wharfs—piers where ships can dock

Index

amphora, 8

animal behavior, 6

Apollo, 10–11

Bay of Naples, 4, 16, 23

colonnade, 5, 10–11, 13–14

earthquakes, 6, 12–13

Herculaneum, 17, 24–25

lapilli, 16–17

lares, 9

lightning, 18–19, 25

Misenum, 16, 20, 22, 25–26

Mount Vesuvius, 4, 7, 13–15, 22, 24, 26

navy, 20

Pliny the Elder, 20, 22–23

Pliny the Younger, 22–23

pyroclastic flow, 15, 25, 27

Romans, 13

Sarno River, 24

Temple of Apollo, 10–11

Temple of Jupiter, 10

Vulcan (Roman god), 6–7

Check It Out!

Books

Lawrence, Caroline. 2010. *The Secrets of Vesuvius*. Orion Children's.

Malam, John. 2008. *You Wouldn't Want to Live in Pompeii! A Volcanic Eruption You'd Rather Avoid*. Franklin Watts.

Shecter, Vicky Alvear. 2014. *Curses and Smoke: A Novel of Pompeii*. Arthur A. Levine Books.

Sonneborn, Liz. 2008. *Pompeii Unearthing Ancient Worlds*. Twenty-First Century Books.

Tanaka, Shelley. 1997. *The Buried City of Pompeii*. Hyperion/Madison Press.

Videos

The History Channel. *Pompeii: The Doomed City*. A&E Home Video.

Peter Nicholson. *Pompeii: The Last Day*. BBC Earth.

Websites

Eyewitness to History. *The Destruction of Pompeii, 79 AD*. http://www.eyewitnesstohistory.com/pompeii.htm.

Live Science. *Mount Vesuvius and Pompeii: Facts & History*. http://www.livescience.com/27871-mount-vesuvius-pompeii.html.

Try It!

You are the writer and publisher of *The Roman News*. After the eruption of Mount Vesuvius, you are in charge of coming up with the front-page layout.

- ◉ In your headline story, include interviews with two eyewitnesses. Use the details from Pliny the Younger's diary on pages 22–23. Provide a detailed description filled with action verbs, adjectives, and adverbs.

- ◉ Include another article speculating why the gods and/or goddesses were angry and made the mountain erupt.

- ◉ Include an advertisement or two that would be found in that area in the year AD 79.

- ◉ Include photos and/or illustrations to bring your story to life. If you're using a computer to complete the newspaper, remember to scan any illustrations you create.

About the Author

Besides writing books for students and conducting training sessions for teachers, Wendy Conklin has a wide variety of interests that include reviving old furniture and competing in rigorous athletic competitions. If there is a challenge, she jumps right in to take it on. Her motto is to live life to the fullest and have no regrets. Someday, she hopes to live in Hawaii, but right now she lives with her family and two sweet Boston terriers in Round Rock, Texas.